HAL•LEONARD

JAZZ PLAY ALONG®

Book and CD for B♭, E♭ and C Instruments

volume 49

BOOK

CD

MILES Davis STANDARDS

10 Jazz Classics

Arranged by Jim Roberts
Produced by Mark Taylor

TITLE	PAGE NUMBERS			
	C Treble Instruments	B♭ Instruments	E♭ Instruments	C Bass Instruments
Autumn Leaves	4	24	44	64
Bye Bye Blackbird	6	26	46	66
Darn That Dream	8	28	48	68
How Deep Is the Ocean (How High Is the Sky)	10	30	50	70
I Loves You, Porgy	12	32	52	72
If I Were a Bell	14	34	54	74
My Funny Valentine	16	36	56	76
On Green Dolphin Street	18	38	58	78
Some Day My Prince Will Come	20	40	60	80
Yesterdays	22	42	62	82

TITLE	CD Track Number Split Track / Melody	CD Track Number Full Stereo Track
Autumn Leaves	1	2
Bye Bye Blackbird	3	4
Darn That Dream	5	6
How Deep Is the Ocean (How High is the Sky)	7	8
I Loves You, Porgy	9	10
If I Were a Bell	11	12
My Funny Valentine	13	14
On Green Dolphin Street	15	16
Some Day My Prince Will Come	17	18
Yesterdays	19	20
B♭ Tuning Notes		21

Photo by William "PoPsie" Randolph
www.PoPsiePhotos.com

ISBN 978-0-634-09077-6

HAL•LEONARD®
CORPORATION

7777 W. BLUEMOUND RD. P.O. BOX 13819 MILWAUKEE, WI 53213

Visit Hal Leonard Online at
www.halleonard.com

Miles Davis Standards

Volume 49

Arranged by Jim Roberts
Produced by Mark Taylor

Featured Players:

Graham Breedlove—Trumpet
Tony Nalker—Piano
Jim Roberts—Bass
Steve Fidyk—Drums

Recorded at Bias Studios, Springfield, Virginia
Bob Dawson, Engineer

HOW TO USE THE CD:

Each song has two tracks:

1) Split Track/Melody

Woodwind, Brass, Keyboard, and **Mallet Players** can use this track as a learning tool for melody style and inflection.

Bass Players can learn and perform with this track – remove the recorded bass track by turning down the volume on the LEFT channel.

Keyboard and **Guitar Players** can learn and perform with this track – remove the recorded piano part by turning down the volume on the RIGHT channel.

2) Full Stereo Track

Soloists or **Groups** can learn and perform with this accompaniment track with the RHYTHM SECTION only.

AUTUMN LEAVES

CD
1: SPLIT TRACK/MELODY
2: FULL STEREO TRACK

C VERSION

ENGLISH LYRIC BY JOHNNY MERCER
FRENCH LYRIC BY JACQUES PREVERT
MUSIC BY JOSEPH KOSMA

Bye Bye Blackbird

LYRIC BY MORT DIXON
MUSIC BY RAY HENDERSON

Darn That Dream

LYRIC BY EDDIE DE LANGE
MUSIC BY JIMMY VAN HEUSEN

C VERSION

9

CD
7 : SPLIT TRACK/MELODY
8 : FULL STEREO TRACK

C VERSION

How Deep Is the Ocean
(How High Is the Sky)

WORDS AND MUSIC BY
IRVING BERLIN

I LOVES YOU, PORGY
FROM PORGY AND BESS

BY GEORGE GERSHWIN,
DU BOSE AND DOROTHY HEYWARD
AND IRA GERSHWIN

C VERSION

IF I WERE A BELL

BY FRANK LOESSER

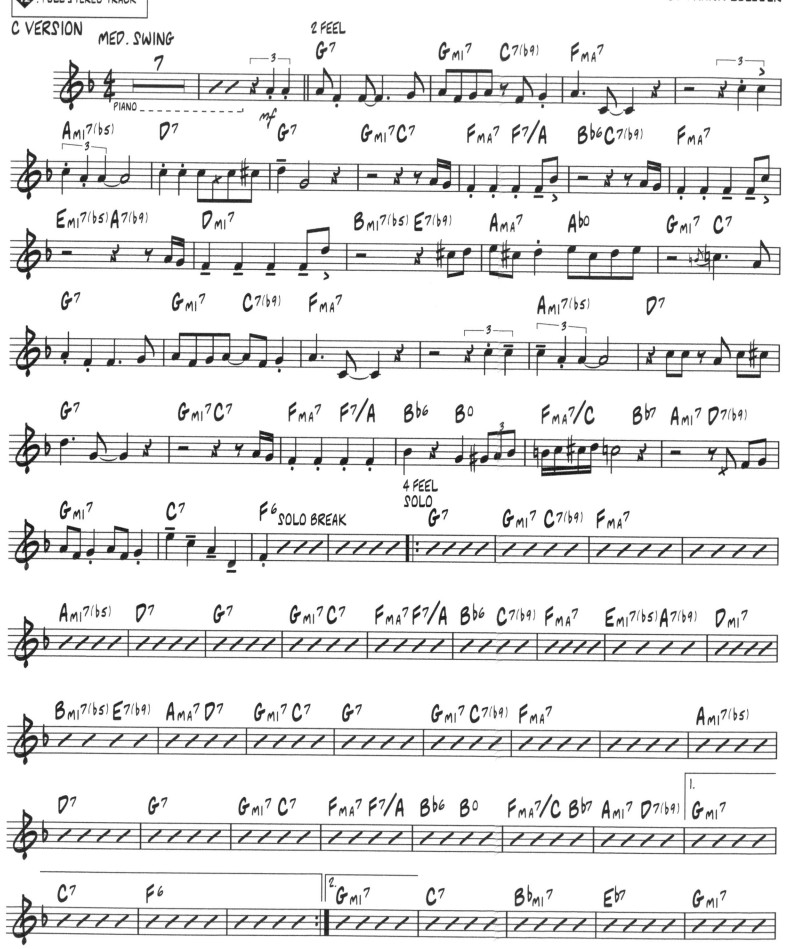

MY FUNNY VALENTINE

CD
13 : SPLIT TRACK/MELODY
14 : FULL STEREO TRACK

WORDS BY LORENZ HART
MUSIC BY RICHARD RODGERS

C VERSION

ON GREEN DOLPHIN STREET

LYRICS BY NED WASHINGTON
MUSIC BY BRONISLAU KAPER

Some Day My Prince Will Come

WORDS BY LARRY MOREY
MUSIC BY FRANK CHURCHILL

C VERSION

YESTERDAYS

WORDS BY OTTO HARBACH
MUSIC BY JEROME KERN

AUTUMN LEAVES

ENGLISH LYRIC BY JOHNNY MERCER
FRENCH LYRIC BY JACQUES PREVERT
MUSIC BY JOSEPH KOSMA

Bye Bye Blackbird

LYRIC BY MORT DIXON
MUSIC BY RAY HENDERSON

27

Darn That Dream

LYRIC BY EDDIE DE LANGE
MUSIC BY JIMMY VAN HEUSEN

Bb VERSION

HOW DEEP IS THE OCEAN
(HOW HIGH IS THE SKY)

WORDS AND MUSIC BY
IRVING BERLIN

Bb VERSION

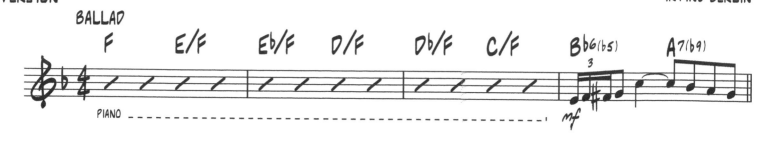

CD

9 : SPLIT TRACK/MELODY
10 : FULL STEREO TRACK

I LOVES YOU, PORGY
FROM PORGY AND BESS

BY GEORGE GERSHWIN,
DU BOSE AND DOROTHY HEYWARD
AND IRA GERSHWIN

Bb VERSION   BALLAD

IF I WERE A BELL

BY FRANK LOESSER

Bb VERSION

My Funny Valentine

WORDS BY LORENZ HART
MUSIC BY RICHARD RODGERS

ON GREEN DOLPHIN STREET

LYRICS BY NED WASHINGTON
MUSIC BY BRONISLAU KAPER

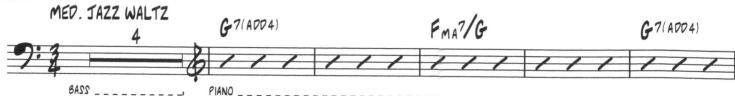

B♭ VERSION

WORDS BY LARRY MOREY
MUSIC BY FRANK CHURCHILL

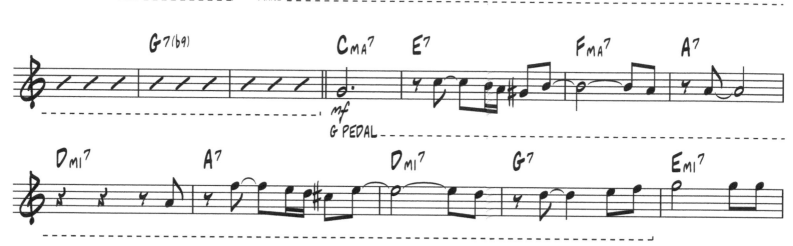

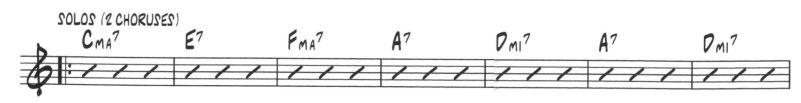

41

Yesterdays

WORDS BY OTTO HARBACH
MUSIC BY JEROME KERN

AUTUMN LEAVES

ENGLISH LYRIC BY JOHNNY MERCER
FRENCH LYRIC BY JACQUES PREVERT
MUSIC BY JOSEPH KOSMA

BYE BYE BLACKBIRD

LYRIC BY MORT DIXON
MUSIC BY RAY HENDERSON

Darn That Dream

Lyric by Eddie De Lange
Music by Jimmy Van Heusen

CD

❼ : SPLIT TRACK/MELODY
❽ : FULL STEREO TRACK

HOW DEEP IS THE OCEAN
(HOW HIGH IS THE SKY)

WORDS AND MUSIC BY
IRVING BERLIN

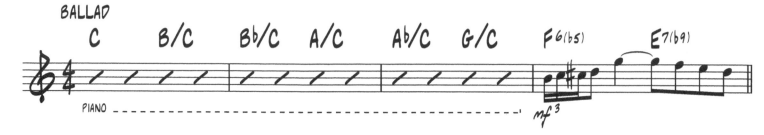

51

I Loves You, Porgy

FROM PORGY AND BESS

BY GEORGE GERSHWIN,
DU BOSE AND DOROTHY HEYWARD
AND IRA GERSHWIN

Eb VERSION

IF I WERE A BELL

BY FRANK LOESSER

Eb VERSION

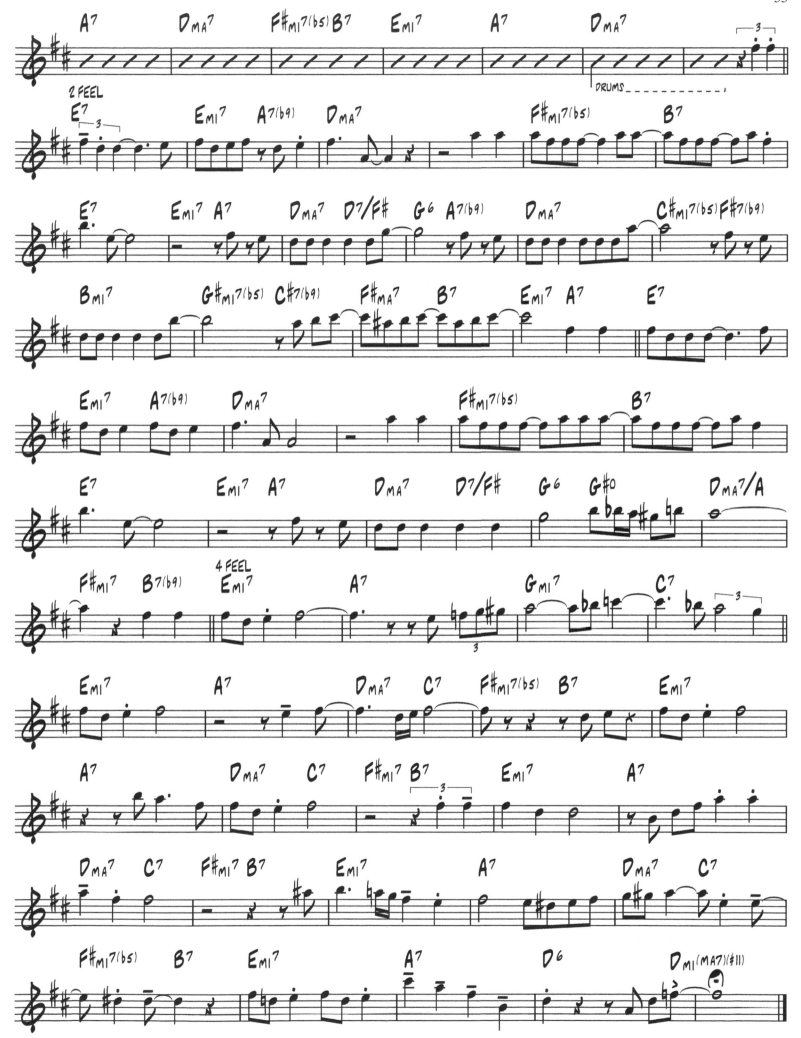

CD

My Funny Valentine

WORDS BY LORENZ HART
MUSIC BY RICHARD RODGERS

CD

15 : SPLIT TRACK/MELODY
16 : FULL STEREO TRACK

On Green Dolphin Street

LYRICS BY NED WASHINGTON
MUSIC BY BRONISLAU KAPER

E♭ VERSION

59

Some Day My Prince Will Come

WORDS BY LARRY MOREY
MUSIC BY FRANK CHURCHILL

Yesterdays

WORDS BY OTTO HARBACH
MUSIC BY JEROME KERN

CD
19 : SPLIT TRACK/MELODY
20 : FULL STEREO TRACK

E♭ VERSION

AUTUMN LEAVES

ENGLISH LYRIC BY JOHNNY MERCER
FRENCH LYRIC BY JACQUES PREVERT
MUSIC BY JOSEPH KOSMA

BYE BYE BLACKBIRD

LYRIC BY MORT DIXON
MUSIC BY RAY HENDERSON

DARN THAT DREAM

LYRIC BY EDDIE DE LANGE
MUSIC BY JIMMY VAN HEUSEN

HOW DEEP IS THE OCEAN
(HOW HIGH IS THE SKY)

WORDS AND MUSIC BY
IRVING BERLIN

C VERSION

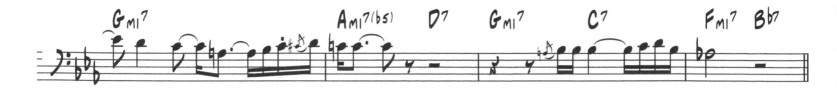

CD
⑨ : SPLIT TRACK/MELODY
⑩ : FULL STEREO TRACK

I LOVES YOU, PORGY
FROM PORGY AND BESS

BY GEORGE GERSHWIN,
DU BOSE AND DOROTHY HEYWARD
AND IRA GERSHWIN

𝄢 C VERSION

IF I WERE A BELL

BY FRANK LOESSER

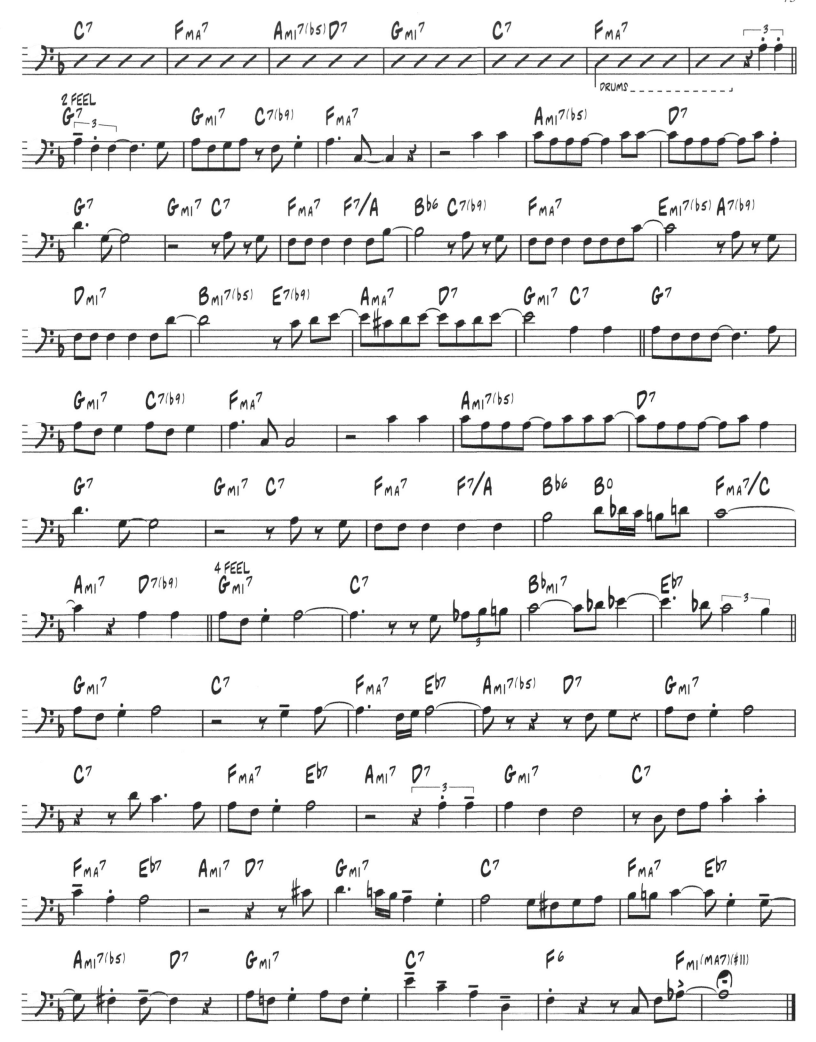

My Funny Valentine

WORDS BY LORENZ HART
MUSIC BY RICHARD RODGERS

On Green Dolphin Street

CD
◆15: SPLIT TRACK/MELODY
◆16: FULL STEREO TRACK

LYRICS BY NED WASHINGTON
MUSIC BY BRONISLAU KAPER

𝄢 C VERSION

Some Day My Prince Will Come

WORDS BY LARRY MOREY
MUSIC BY FRANK CHURCHILL

C VERSION

Yesterdays

WORDS BY OTTO HARBACH
MUSIC BY JEROME KERN

Presenting the Hal Leonard JAZZ PLAY-ALONG SERIES

1. DUKE ELLINGTON
00841644 .... $16.95

1A. MAIDEN VOYAGE/ALL BLUES
00843158 .... $15.99

2. MILES DAVIS
00841645 .... $16.95

3. THE BLUES
00841646 .... $16.99

4. JAZZ BALLADS
00841691 .... $16.99

5. BEST OF BEBOP
00841689 .... $16.99

6. JAZZ CLASSICS WITH EASY CHANGES
00841690 .... $16.99

7. ESSENTIAL JAZZ STANDARDS
00843000 .... $16.99

8. ANTONIO CARLOS JOBIM AND THE ART OF THE BOSSA NOVA
00843001 .... $16.95

9. DIZZY GILLESPIE
00843002 .... $16.99

10. DISNEY CLASSICS
00843003 .... $16.99

11. RODGERS AND HART – FAVORITES
00843004 .... $16.99

12. ESSENTIAL JAZZ CLASSICS
00843005 .... $16.99

13. JOHN COLTRANE
00843006 .... $16.95

14. IRVING BERLIN
00843007 .... $15.99

15. RODGERS & HAMMERSTEIN
00843008 .... $15.99

16. COLE PORTER
00843009 .... $15.95

17. COUNT BASIE
00843010 .... $16.95

18. HAROLD ARLEN
00843011 .... $15.95

19. COOL JAZZ
00843012 .... $15.95

20. CHRISTMAS CAROLS
00843080 .... $14.95

21. RODGERS AND HART – CLASSICS
00843014 .... $14.95

22. WAYNE SHORTER
00843015 .... $16.95

23. LATIN JAZZ
00843016 .... $16.95

24. EARLY JAZZ STANDARDS
00843017 .... $14.95

25. CHRISTMAS JAZZ
00843018 .... $16.95

26. CHARLIE PARKER
00843019 .... $16.95

27. GREAT JAZZ STANDARDS
00843020 .... $15.99

28. BIG BAND ERA
00843021 .... $15.99

29. LENNON AND McCARTNEY
00843022 .... $16.95

30. BLUES' BEST
00843023 .... $15.99

31. JAZZ IN THREE
00843024 .... $15.99

32. BEST OF SWING
00843025 .... $15.99

33. SONNY ROLLINS
00843029 .... $15.95

34. ALL TIME STANDARDS
00843030 .... $15.99

35. BLUESY JAZZ
00843031 .... $15.99

36. HORACE SILVER
00843032 .... $16.99

37. BILL EVANS
00843033 .... $16.95

38. YULETIDE JAZZ
00843034 .... $16.95

39. "ALL THE THINGS YOU ARE" & MORE JEROME KERN SONGS
00843035 .... $15.99

40. BOSSA NOVA
00843036 .... $15.99

41. CLASSIC DUKE ELLINGTON
00843037 .... $16.99

42. GERRY MULLIGAN – FAVORITES
00843038 .... $16.99

43. GERRY MULLIGAN – CLASSICS
00843039 .... $16.95

44. OLIVER NELSON
00843040 .... $16.95

45. JAZZ AT THE MOVIES
00843041 .... $15.99

46. BROADWAY JAZZ STANDARDS
00843042 .... $15.99

47. CLASSIC JAZZ BALLADS
00843043 .... $15.99

48. BEBOP CLASSICS
00843044 .... $16.99

49. MILES DAVIS – STANDARDS
00843045 .... $16.95

50. GREAT JAZZ CLASSICS
00843046 .... $15.99

51. UP-TEMPO JAZZ
00843047 .... $15.99

52. STEVIE WONDER
00843048 .... $15.95

53. RHYTHM CHANGES
00843049 .... $15.99

54. "MOONLIGHT IN VERMONT" & OTHER GREAT STANDARDS
00843050 .... $15.99

55. BENNY GOLSON
00843052 .... $15.95

56. "GEORGIA ON MY MIND" & OTHER SONGS BY HOAGY CARMICHAEL
00843056 .... $15.99

57. VINCE GUARALDI
00843057 .... $16.99

58. MORE LENNON AND McCARTNEY
00843059 .... $15.99

59. SOUL JAZZ
00843060 .... $15.99

60. DEXTER GORDON
00843061 .... $15.95

61. MONGO SANTAMARIA
00843062 .... $15.95

62. JAZZ-ROCK FUSION
00843063 .... $14.95

63. CLASSICAL JAZZ
00843064 .... $14.95

64. TV TUNES
00843065 .... $14.95

65. SMOOTH JAZZ
00843066 .... $16.99

66. A CHARLIE BROWN CHRISTMAS
00843067 .... $16.99

67. CHICK COREA
00843068 .... $15.95

68. CHARLES MINGUS
00843069 .... $16.95

69. CLASSIC JAZZ
00843071 .... $15.99

70. THE DOORS
00843072 .... $14.95

71. COLE PORTER CLASSICS
00843073 .... $14.95

72. CLASSIC JAZZ BALLADS
00843074 .... $15.99

73. JAZZ/BLUES
00843075 .... $14.95

74. BEST JAZZ CLASSICS
00843076 .... $15.99

75. PAUL DESMOND
00843077 .... $14.95

76. BROADWAY JAZZ BALLADS
00843078 .... $15.99

77. JAZZ ON BROADWAY
00843079 .... $15.99

78. STEELY DAN
00843070 .... $14.99

79. MILES DAVIS – CLASSICS
00843081 .... $15.99

80. JIMI HENDRIX
00843083 .... $15.99

81. FRANK SINATRA – CLASSICS
00843084 .... $15.99

82. FRANK SINATRA – STANDARDS
00843085 .... $15.99

83. ANDREW LLOYD WEBBER
00843104 .... $14.95

84. BOSSA NOVA CLASSICS
00843105 .... $14.95

85. MOTOWN HITS
00843109 .... $14.95

86. BENNY GOODMAN
00843110 .... $14.95

87. DIXIELAND
00843111 .... $14.95

88. DUKE ELLINGTON FAVORITES
00843112 .... $14.95

89. IRVING BERLIN FAVORITES
00843113 .... $14.95

90. THELONIOUS MONK CLASSICS
00841262 .... $16.99

91. THELONIOUS MONK FAVORITES
00841263 .... $16.99

92. LEONARD BERNSTEIN
00450134 .... $15.99

93. DISNEY FAVORITES
00843142 .... $14.99

94. RAY
00843143 .... $14.99

95. JAZZ AT THE LOUNGE
00843144 .... $14.99

96. LATIN JAZZ STANDARDS
00843145 .... $14.99

97. MAYBE I'M AMAZED
00843148 .... $15.99

98. DAVE FRISHBERG
00843149 .... $15.99

99. SWINGING STANDARDS
00843150 .... $14.99

100. LOUIS ARMSTRONG
00740423 .... $15.99

101. BUD POWELL
00843152 .... $14.99

102. JAZZ POP
00843153 .... $14.99

103. ON GREEN DOLPHIN STREET & OTHER JAZZ CLASSICS
00843154 .... $14.99

104. ELTON JOHN
00843155 .... $14.99

105. SOULFUL JAZZ
00843151 .... $15.99

106. SLO' JAZZ
00843117 .... $14.99

107. MOTOWN CLASSICS
00843116 .... $14.99

108. JAZZ WALTZ
00843159 .... $15.99

109. OSCAR PETERSON
00843160 .... $15.99

110. JUST STANDARDS
00843161 .... $15.99

111. COOL CHRISTMAS
00843162 .... $15.99

114. MODERN JAZZ QUARTET FAVORITES
00843163 .... $15.99

115. THE SOUND OF MUSIC
00843164 .... $15.99

116. JACO PASTORIUS
00843165 .... $15.99

117. ANTONIO CARLOS JOBIM – MORE HITS
00843166 .... $15.99

118. BIG JAZZ STANDARDS COLLECTION
00843167 .... $27.50

119. JELLY ROLL MORTON
00843168 .... $15.99

120. J.S. BACH
00843169 .... $15.99

121. DJANGO REINHARDT
00843170 .... $15.99

122. PAUL SIMON
00843182 .... $16.99

123. BACHARACH & DAVID
00843185 .... $15.99

124. JAZZ-ROCK HORN HITS
00843186 .... $15.99

126. COUNT BASIE CLASSICS
00843157 .... $15.99

HAL•LEONARD®
CORPORATION
7777 W. BLUEMOUND RD. P.O. BOX 13819
MILWAUKEE, WISCONSIN 53213

Visit Hal Leonard online at
www.halleonard.com
for complete songlists.

0910

The Best-Selling Jazz Book of All Time Is Now Legal!

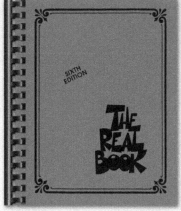

The Real Books are the most popular jazz books of all time. Since the 1970s, musicians have trusted these volumes to get them through every gig, night after night. The problem is that the books were illegally produced and distributed, without any regard to copyright law, or royalties paid to the composers who created these musical masterpieces.

Hal Leonard is very proud to present the first legitimate and legal editions of these books ever produced. You won't even notice the difference, other than all the notorious errors being fixed: the covers and typeface look the same, the song lists are nearly identical, and the price for our edition is even cheaper than the originals!

Every conscientious musician will appreciate that these books are now produced accurately and ethically, benefitting the songwriters that we owe for some of the greatest tunes of all time!

VOLUME 1
00240221	C Edition	$39.99
00240224	Bb Edition	$39.99
00240225	Eb Edition	$39.99
00240226	Bass Clef Edition	$39.99
00286389	F Edition	$39.99
00240292	C Edition 6 x 9	$35.00
00240339	Bb Edition 6 x 9	$35.00
00147792	Bass Clef Edition 6 x 9	$35.00
00451087	C Edition on CD-ROM	$29.99
00200984	Online Backing Tracks: Selections	$45.00
00110604	Book/USB Flash Drive Backing Tracks Pack	$79.99
00110599	USB Flash Drive Only	$50.00

VOLUME 2
00240222	C Edition	$39.99
00240227	Bb Edition	$39.99
00240228	Eb Edition	$39.99
00240229	Bass Clef Edition	$39.99
00240293	C Edition 6 x 9	$35.00
00125900	Bb Edition 6 x 9	$35.00
00451088	C Edition on CD-ROM	$30.99
00125900	The Real Book – Mini Edition	$35.00
00204126	Backing Tracks on USB Flash Drive	$50.00
00204131	C Edition – USB Flash Drive Pack	$79.99

VOLUME 3
00240233	C Edition	$39.99
00240284	Bb Edition	$39.99
00240285	Eb Edition	$39.99
00240286	Bass Clef Edition	$39.99
00240338	C Edition 6 x 9	$35.00
00451089	C Edition on CD-ROM	$29.99

VOLUME 4
00240296	C Edition	$39.99
00103348	Bb Edition	$39.99
00103349	Eb Edition	$39.99
00103350	Bass Clef Edition	$39.99

VOLUME 5
00240349	C Edition	$39.99
00175278	Bb Edition	$39.99
00175279	Eb Edition	$39.99

VOLUME 6
00240534	C Edition	$39.99
00223637	Eb Edition	$39.99

Also available:
00154230	The Real Bebop Book	$34.99
00240264	The Real Blues Book	$34.99
00310910	The Real Bluegrass Book	$35.00
00240223	The Real Broadway Book	$35.00
00240440	The Trane Book	$22.99
00125426	The Real Country Book	$39.99
00269721	The Real Miles Davis Book C Edition	$24.99
00269723	The Real Miles Davis Book Bb Edition	$24.99
00240355	The Real Dixieland Book C Edition	$32.50
00294853	The Real Dixieland Book Eb Edition	$35.00
00122335	The Real Dixieland Book Bb Edition	$35.00
00240235	The Duke Ellington Real Book	$22.99
00240268	The Real Jazz Solos Book	$30.00
00240348	The Real Latin Book C Edition	$37.50
00127107	The Real Latin Book Bb Edition	$35.00
00120809	The Pat Metheny Real Book C Edition	$27.50
00252119	The Pat Metheny Real Book Bb Edition	$24.99
00240358	The Charlie Parker Real Book C Edition	$19.99
00275997	The Charlie Parker Real Book Eb Edition	$19.99
00118324	The Real Pop Book – Vol. 1	$35.00
00240331	The Bud Powell Real Book	$19.99
00240437	The Real R&B Book C Edition	$39.99
00276590	The Real R&B Book Bb Edition	$39.99
00240313	The Real Rock Book	$35.00
00240323	The Real Rock Book – Vol. 2	$35.00
00240359	The Real Tab Book	$32.50
00240317	The Real Worship Book	$29.99

THE REAL CHRISTMAS BOOK
00240306	C Edition	$32.50
00240345	Bb Edition	$32.50
00240346	Eb Edition	$35.00
00240347	Bass Clef Edition	$32.50
00240431	A-G CD Backing Tracks	$24.99
00240432	H-M CD Backing Tracks	$24.99
00240433	N-Y CD Backing Tracks	$24.99

THE REAL VOCAL BOOK
00240230	Volume 1 High Voice	$35.00
00240307	Volume 1 Low Voice	$35.00
00240231	Volume 2 High Voice	$35.00
00240308	Volume 2 Low Voice	$35.00
00240391	Volume 3 High Voice	$35.00
00240392	Volume 3 Low Voice	$35.00
00118318	Volume 4 High Voice	$35.00
00118319	Volume 4 Low Voice	$35.00

Complete song lists online at www.halleonard.com

Prices, content, and availability subject to change without notice.

JAZZ INSTRUCTION & IMPROVISATION

BOOKS FOR ALL INSTRUMENTS FROM HAL LEONARD

500 JAZZ LICKS
by Brent Vaartstra
This book aims to assist you on your journey to play jazz fluently. These short phrases and ideas we call "licks" will help you understand how to navigate the common chords and chord progressions you will encounter. Adding this vocabulary to your arsenal will send you down the right path and improve your jazz playing, regardless of your instrument.
00142384 ....$16.99

1001 JAZZ LICKS
by Jack Shneidman
Cherry Lane Music
This book presents 1,001 melodic gems played over dozens of the most important chord progressions heard in jazz. This is the ideal book for beginners seeking a well-organized, easy-to-follow encyclopedia of jazz vocabulary, as well as professionals who want to take their knowledge of the jazz language to new heights.
02500133 ....$14.99

THE BERKLEE BOOK OF JAZZ HARMONY
by Joe Mulholland & Tom Hojnacki
Learn jazz harmony, as taught at Berklee College of Music. This text provides a strong foundation in harmonic principles, supporting further study in jazz composition, arranging, and improvisation. It covers basic chord types and their tensions, with practical demonstrations of how they are used in characteristic jazz contexts and an accompanying recording that lets you hear how they can be applied.
00113755 Book/Online Audio.................................$19.99

BUILDING A JAZZ VOCABULARY
By Mike Steinel
A valuable resource for learning the basics of jazz from Mike Steinel of the University of North Texas. It covers: the basics of jazz • how to build effective solos • a comprehensive practice routine • and a jazz vocabulary of the masters.
00849911 ....$19.99

COMPREHENSIVE TECHNIQUE FOR JAZZ MUSICIANS
2ND EDITION
by Bert Ligon
Houston Publishing
An incredible presentation of the most practical exercises an aspiring jazz student could want. All are logically interwoven with fine "real world" examples from jazz to classical. This book is an essential anthology of technical, compositional, and theoretical exercises, with lots of musical examples.
00030455 ....$34.99

EAR TRAINING
by Keith Wyatt,
Carl Schroeder and Joe Elliott
Musicians Institute Press
Covers: basic pitch matching • singing major and minor scales • identifying intervals • transcribing melodies and rhythm • identifying chords and progressions • seventh chords and the blues • modal interchange, chromaticism, modulation • and more.
00695198 Book/Online Audio.................................$24.99

EXERCISES AND ETUDES FOR THE JAZZ INSTRUMENTALIST
by J.J. Johnson
Designed as study material and playable by any instrument, these pieces run the gamut of the jazz experience, featuring common and uncommon time signatures and keys, and styles from ballads to funk. They are progressively graded so that both beginners and professionals will be challenged by the demands of this wonderful music.
00842018 Bass Clef Edition.................................$19.99
00842042 Treble Clef Edition...............................$16.95

HOW TO PLAY FROM A REAL BOOK
by Robert Rawlins
Explore, understand, and perform the songs in real books with the techniques in this book. Learn how to analyze the form and harmonic structure, insert an introduction, interpret the melody, improvise on the chords, construct bass lines, voice the chords, add substitutions, and more. It addresses many aspects of solo and small band performance that can improve your own playing and your understanding of what others are doing around you.
00312097 ....$19.99

JAZZ DUETS
ETUDES FOR PHRASING AND ARTICULATION
by Richard Lowell
Berklee Press
With these 27 duets in jazz and jazz-influenced styles, you will learn how to improve your ear, sense of timing, phrasing, and your facility in bringing theoretical principles into musical expression. Covers: jazz staccato & legato • scales, modes & harmonies • phrasing within and between measures • swing feel • and more.
00302151 ....$14.99

JAZZ THEORY & WORKBOOK
by Lilian Dericq &
Étienne Guéreau
Designed for all instrumentalists, this book teaches how jazz standards are constructed. It is also a great resource for arrangers and composers seeking new writing tools. While some of the musical examples are pianistic, this book is not exclusively for keyboard players.
00159022 ....$19.99

JAZZ THEORY RESOURCES
by Bert Ligon
Houston Publishing, Inc.
This is a jazz theory text in two volumes. **Volume 1 includes**: review of basic theory • rhythm in jazz performance • triadic generalization • diatonic harmonic progressions and analysis • substitutions and turnarounds • and more. **Volume 2 includes**: modes and modal frameworks • quartal harmony • extended tertian structures and triadic superimposition • pentatonic applications • coloring "outside" the lines and beyond • and more.
00030458 Volume 1.....................................$39.99
00030459 Volume 2.....................................$32.99

JAZZOLOGY
THE ENCYCLOPEDIA OF JAZZ THEORY FOR ALL MUSICIANS
by Robert Rawlins and
Nor Eddine Bahha
This comprehensive resource covers a variety of jazz topics, for beginners and pros of any instrument. The book serves as an encyclopedia for reference, a thorough methodology for the student, and a workbook for the classroom.
00311167 ....$24.99

MODALOGY
SCALES, MODES & CHORDS: THE PRIMORDIAL BUILDING BLOCKS OF MUSIC
by Jeff Brent with Schell Barkley
Primarily a music theory reference, this book presents a unique perspective on the origins, interlocking aspects, and usage of the most common scales and modes in occidental music. Anyone wishing to seriously explore the realms of scales, modes, and their real-world functions will find the most important issues dealt with in meticulous detail within these pages.
00312274 ....$24.99

THE SOURCE
THE DICTIONARY OF CONTEMPORARY AND TRADITIONAL SCALES
by Steve Barta
This book serves as an informative guide for people who are looking for good, solid information regarding scales, chords, and how they work together. It provides right and left hand fingerings for scales, chords, and complete inversions. Includes over 20 different scales, each written in all 12 keys.
00240885 ....$19.99

www.halleonard.com

A R T I S T
TRANSCRIPTIONS®

Artist Transcriptions are authentic, note-for-note transcriptions of today's hottest artists in jazz, pop and rock. These outstanding, accurate arrangements are in an easy-to-read format which includes all essential lines. Artist Transcriptions can be used to perform, sequence or for reference.

CLARINET
00672423 Buddy De Franco Collection $19.95

FLUTE
00672379 Eric Dolphy Collection.................$19.95
00672582 The Very Best of James Galway .$19.99
00672372 James Moody Collection –
Sax and Flute $19.95

GUITAR & BASS
00660113 Guitar Style of George Benson....$19.99
00672573 Ray Brown –
Legendary Jazz Bassist............. $22.99
00672331 Ron Carter Collection..................$19.99
00660115 Al Di Meola –
Friday Night in San Francisco..... $17.99
00604043 Al Di Meola –
Music, Words, Pictures $14.95
00125617 Best of Herb Ellis $19.99
00673245 Jazz Style of Tal Farlow $24.99
00699306 Jim Hall – Exploring Jazz Guitar ..$19.99
00672353 The Joe Pass Collection $19.99
00673216 John Patitucci............................ $17.99
00672374 Johnny Smith – Guitar Solos...... $24.99
00672320 Mark Whitfield Guitar Collection ..$19.95

PIANO & KEYBOARD
00672338 The Monty Alexander Collection .$19.95
00672487 Monty Alexander Plays Standards $19.95
00672520 Count Basie Collection $19.95
00192307 Bebop Piano Legends.................$19.99
00113680 Blues Piano Legends..................$22.99
00672526 The Bill Charlap Collection......... $19.99
00278003 A Charlie Brown Christmas........ $17.99
00672439 Cyrus Chestnut Collection $19.95
00672300 Chick Corea – Paint the World....$19.99
00146105 Bill Evans – Alone....................... $19.99
00672548 The Mastery of Bill Evans $16.99
00672425 Bill Evans – Piano Interpretations $22.99
00672365 Bill Evans – Play Standards....... $22.99
00121885 Bill Evans – Time Remembered ..$19.99
00672510 Bill Evans Trio Vol. 1: 1959-1961 .$27.99
00672511 Bill Evans Trio Vol. 2: 1962-1965.. $27.99
00672512 Bill Evans Trio Vol. 3: 1968-1974. $29.99
00672513 Bill Evans Trio Vol. 4: 1979-1980. $24.95
00193332 Erroll Garner –
Concert by the Sea................... $22.99
00672486 Vince Guaraldi Collection............$19.99
00289644 The Definitive Vince Guaraldi..... $34.99
00672419 Herbie Hancock Collection......... $22.99
00672438 Hampton Hawes Collection.........$19.95

00672322 Ahmad Jamal Collection $24.99
00255671 Jazz Piano Masterpieces.............$19.99
00124367 Jazz Piano Masters Play
Rodgers & Hammerstein $19.99
00672564 Best of Jeff Lorber...................... $19.99
00672476 Brad Mehldau Collection............ $22.99
00672388 Best of Thelonious Monk $22.99
00672389 Thelonious Monk Collection....... $24.99
00672390 Thelonious Monk Plays
Jazz Standards – Volume 1 .... $22.99
00672391 Thelonious Monk Plays
Jazz Standards – Volume 2 .... $22.99
00672433 Jelly Roll Morton –
The Piano Rolls $17.99
00672553 Charlie Parker Piano featuring
The Paul Smith Trio (Book/CD)..$19.95
00264094 Oscar Peterson – Night Train $19.99
00672544 Oscar Peterson – Originals.........$14.99
00672531 Oscar Peterson –
Plays Duke Ellington $24.99
00672563 Oscar Peterson –
A Royal Wedding Suite $19.99
00672569 Oscar Peterson – Tracks $19.99
00672533 Oscar Peterson – Trios................ $29.99
00672534 Very Best of Oscar Peterson...... $22.95
00672371 Bud Powell Classics................... $22.99
00672376 Bud Powell Collection $24.99
00672507 Gonzalo Rubalcaba Collection ...$19.95
00672303 Horace Silver Collection............. $24.99
00672316 Art Tatum Collection $24.99
00672355 Art Tatum Solo Book $19.99
00672357 The Billy Taylor Collection $24.95
00673215 McCoy Tyner $22.99
00672321 Cedar Walton Collection $19.95
00672519 Kenny Werner Collection.............$19.95
00672434 Teddy Wilson Collection $22.99

SAXOPHONE
00672566 The Mindi Abair Collection $14.99
00673244 Julian "Cannonball"
Adderley Collection.................... $22.99
00673237 Michael Brecker $19.99
00672429 Michael Brecker Collection $24.99
00672394 James Carter Collection..............$19.95
00672529 John Coltrane – Giant Steps.......$17.99
00672494 John Coltrane – A Love Supreme$16.99
00672493 John Coltrane Plays
"Coltrane Changes"....................$19.95
00672453 John Coltrane Plays Standards.. $24.99
00673233 John Coltrane Solos $27.99
00672328 Paul Desmond Collection............$19.99
00672530 Kenny Garrett Collection $22.99

00699375 Stan Getz....................................$19.99
00672377 Stan Getz – Bossa Novas $22.99
00672375 Stan Getz – Standards $19.99
00673254 Great Tenor Sax Solos............... $22.99
00672523 Coleman Hawkins Collection $22.99
00672330 Best of Joe Henderson $24.99
00673239 Best of Kenny G.......................... $22.99
00673229 Kenny G – Breathless $19.99
00672462 Kenny G –
Classics in the Key of G............. $22.99
00672485 Kenny G – Faith: A Holiday Album. $17.99
00672373 Kenny G – The Moment.............$19.99
00672498 Jackie McLean Collection $19.95
00672372 James Moody Collection –
Sax and Flute $19.95
00672416 Frank Morgan Collection $19.95
00672539 Gerry Mulligan Collection........... $22.99
00672561 Best of Sonny Rollins..................$19.95
00102751 Sonny Rollins, Art Blakey & Kenny Drew
with the Modern Jazz Quartet $17.95
00675000 David Sanborn Collection $19.99
00672528 The Bud Shank Collection $19.99
00672491 The New Best of Wayne Shorter $24.99
00672550 The Sonny Stitt Collection...........$19.95
00672524 Lester Young Collection...............$19.99

TROMBONE
00672332 J.J. Johnson Collection $22.99
00672489 Steve Turré Collection $19.99

TRUMPET
00672557 Herb Alpert Collection................ $19.99
00672480 Louis Armstrong Collection $19.99
00672481 Louis Armstrong Plays Standards$19.99
00672435 Chet Baker Collection $22.99
00672556 Best of Chris Botti $19.99
00672448 Miles Davis – Originals, Vol. 1 .....$19.99
00672451 Miles Davis – Originals, Vol. 2 .....$19.95
00672449 Miles Davis – Standards, Vol. 2...$19.95
00672479 Dizzy Gillespie Collection $19.95
00673214 Freddie Hubbard $19.99
00672506 Chuck Mangione Collection $19.99
00672525 Arturo Sandoval –
Trumpet Evolution $19.99

HAL•LEONARD®